A TRUE BOOK™

Sam Walton
Rethinking Retail

WIL MARA

Children's Press®
An Imprint of Scholastic Inc.
New York Toronto London Auckland Sydney
Mexico City New Delhi Hong Kong
Danbury, Connecticut

D1194797

Content Consultant
James Marten, PhD
Professor and Chair, History Department
Marquette University
Milwaukee, Wisconsin

Library of Congress Cataloging-in-Publication Data
Mara, Wil.
  Sam Walton : rethinking retail / Wil Mara.
     pages cm.—(A true book)
  Includes bibliographical references and index.
  ISBN 978-0-531-24778-5 (lib. bdg.) — ISBN 978-0-531-28464-3 (pbk.)
1. Walton, Sam, 1918–1992—Juvenile literature. 2. Businesspeople—United States—Biography—
Juvenile literature. 3. Millionaires—United States—Biography—Juvenile literature. 4. Wal-Mart
(Firm)—History—Juvenile literature. 5. Discount houses (Retail trade)—United States—History—
Juvenile literature. I. Title.
  HC102.5.W35M37 2014
  381'.149092—dc23[B]   2013001210

No part of this publication may be reproduced in whole or in part, or stored in a retrieval system,
or transmitted in any form or by any means, electronic, mechanical, photocopying, recording, or
otherwise, without written permission of the publisher. For information regarding permission,
write to Scholastic Inc., Attention: Permissions Department, 557 Broadway, New York, NY 10012.
© 2014 Scholastic Inc.

All rights reserved. Published in 2014 by Children's Press, an imprint of Scholastic Inc.
Printed in China 62
SCHOLASTIC, CHILDREN'S PRESS, A TRUE BOOK™, and associated logos are trademarks and/or
registered trademarks of Scholastic Inc.
1 2 3 4 5 6 7 8 9 10 R 23 22 21 20 19 18 17 16 15 14

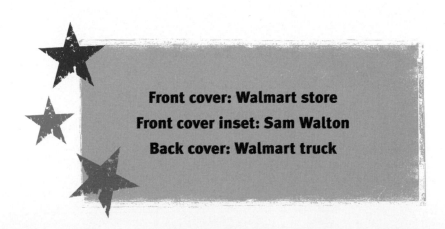

Front cover: Walmart store
Front cover inset: Sam Walton
Back cover: Walmart truck

Find the Truth!

Everything you are about to read is true *except* for one of the sentences on this page.

Which one is **TRUE**?

T or F Sam Walton once worked for J. C. Penney.

T or F Sam Walton launched the retail chains Walmart, Sam's Club, and Target.

Find the answers in this book.

Contents

THE BIG TRUTH!

Groundbreaking Ideas in Retail

Walton specialized in running variety and discount stores.

Walton ran Walmart for more than 25 years.

NEBRASKA

Omaha

Lincoln ★

IOWA

ILLINOIS

Springfield ★

Shelbina

Kansas City

Columbia

Topeka ★

Marshall

KANSAS

Springfield

Jefferson City

St. Louis

MISSOURI

Wichita

Kingfisher

Oklahoma City ★

OKLAHOMA

Arkansas River

ARKANSAS

Little Rock ★

Mississippi River

TEXAS

N
W ● E
S

MISSISSIPPI

0   miles   200

0   km   200

6

A Hardworking Boy

Samuel Moore Walton was born on March 29, 1918, in the small farming town of Kingfisher, Oklahoma. When he was five years old, his family moved to Missouri, where he grew up. Sam had just one sibling, his brother, James, who was born in 1921. James would eventually become known by the nickname Bud. He and Sam grew to be very close.

The Waltons had lived in four different Missouri towns by the time Sam went to college.

Learning the Value of a Dollar

Sam came to understand the importance of money very early in life. His father worked day after day on the family farm but barely managed to cover the family's living **expenses**. Sam helped out where he could. He would get up very early to help his father or to milk the cows. He also made milk deliveries after school, while other boys were out playing with their friends.

Like these farmers, Sam Walton helped his family make money by selling milk from their cows.

Unemployed men waited in long lines for hot meals during the Great Depression.

Sam also earned money selling magazine subscriptions and delivering newspapers. This was his way of making the most of what little spare time he had. When the **Great Depression** struck in 1929, millions of people lost everything they had. This deepened Sam's sense of how important it was to have enough money.

Sam was voted the "most versatile boy" in his graduating class.

School Days

Just as Sam worked hard for his family at home, he worked hard when he was at school. He had a friendly, outgoing personality that made him popular with the other students. He liked sports because he liked to compete—and especially to win. This drive to be a winner would last throughout his life. In high school, Sam played football and became the team's quarterback.

Sam's parents had always encouraged Sam and his brother to attend college. The family even moved to Columbia, Missouri, in Sam's sophomore year of high school to be near the town's many schools. Sam chose the University of Missouri in Columbia. His college education cost more than his family could pay. Sam took various jobs to cover the cost of his education. He continued to sell magazine subscriptions. He also worked in a restaurant and as a lifeguard.

Sam was extremely active in college, participating in sports and clubs in addition to working at jobs and doing schoolwork.

CHAPTER 2

The Art of Selling Things

Walton graduated from the University of Missouri in 1940 with a degree in **economics**. He considered becoming a salesman in the insurance business. He also thought about continuing his education at the famous Wharton School of Finance in Pennsylvania, though it would be difficult to afford. But overall, he just wasn't sure what he wanted to do next.

Walton was voted class president in high school and in college.

Working Retail

With his future plans uncertain, Walton pursued a job in the **retail** business. He met with representatives from J. C. Penney and Sears, two of the most popular retail stores in the world. Both were looking to hire young and talented people. Walton impressed both companies enough for them to offer him jobs. He eventually took the position with J. C. Penney.

J. C. Penney stores such as this one in Minneapolis, Minnesota, have long been located across the United States.

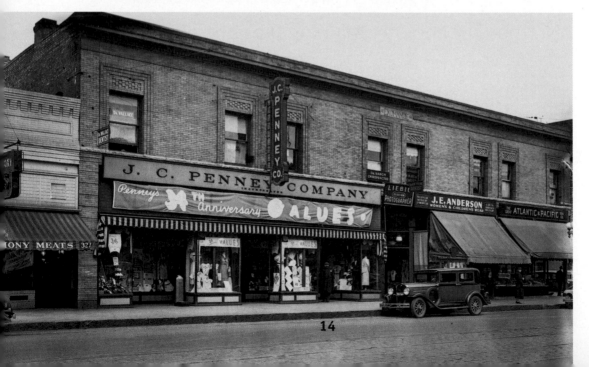

Walton was one of the 16 million U.S. soldiers who fought in World War II.

Walton worked hard at J. C. Penney. He moved to Iowa to train as a manager and run a store. He was an excellent salesman who loved dealing with customers.

In 1942, he met a woman named Helen Robson. They were married the following year and started a family soon after. Their son Rob was born in 1944. John, Jim, and Alice were born over the next few years.

Ben Franklin stores were originally founded by brothers Edward and George Butler.

A Store of His Own

As much as he enjoyed his job, Walton gave it up soon after getting married so he could join the military during World War II (1939–1945). When Walton finished his military service in 1945, he was eager to get back to the retail business. This time, however, he didn't want to work for someone else—he wanted his own store. He decided to **invest** in the Ben Franklin **chain** of retail stores. Ben Franklin stores were similar to J. C. Penney stores. They sold many different items in one location. Walton liked this approach very much.

A Penny Saved Is a Penny Earned

The Ben Franklin chain of discount stores began as a mail-order business in 1877. The store's marketing honored Benjamin Franklin's famous saying, "A penny saved is a penny earned." There were more than 2,500 Ben Franklin stores years ago, but today few remain. Ben Franklin lost many of its customers to other discount chains, such as Kmart, Target, and the one that Sam Walton would eventually launch—Walmart.

The Ben Franklin **franchise** that Walton wanted was in Newport, Arkansas. He needed $25,000 to purchase it. He had already saved about $5,000, and he borrowed the rest from his father-in-law. The store's previous owner was happy to get rid of it. It was not making much money, mainly because it couldn't keep up with a competing retail store right across the street. But Walton had ideas that would turn the Ben Franklin into a winner.

Ben Franklin and other retail stores are sometimes called variety stores because of the variety of products they offer.

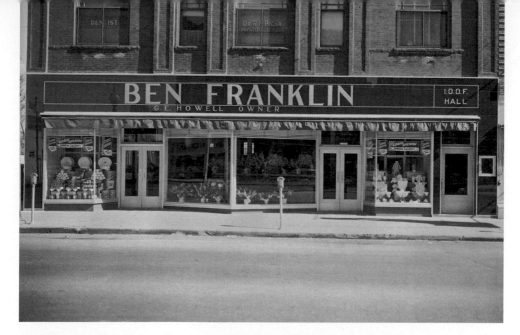

Chains such as Ben Franklin often require all franchise owners to follow a set of rules when running their businesses.

Breaking the Rules

Soon after Walton took over the Ben Franklin in Newport, he discovered a huge problem standing in the way of his success. The people who owned the Ben Franklin chain had a certain way of doing things. Walton didn't always agree with their methods. When he thought of better ways to make money for the store, he ignored the company's rules and did things his own way.

Stores that sell goods at low prices can make more money by making many small sales instead of a few large ones.

Low, Low Prices

If Walton wanted to sell a certain item, he was supposed to buy it at a set price from Ben Franklin's main supplier. But sometimes he found out where Ben Franklin was getting the item. He then went straight to the source and bought the item for a lower price. This allowed him to sell things cheaper. Soon, his store was making more money than his competitor across the street.

Moving On

In spite of Walton's success with the Ben Franklin in Newport, he was forced to give up the store after just five years. Another person owned the property where the store was located and refused to renew Walton's rental agreement. Walton was disappointed, but he believed that he could use what he had learned at Ben Franklin to do something even better.

Small store owners often lease space from landlords instead of owning their own buildings.

Sam Walton's desk at his Bentonville, Arkansas, store is preserved today as part of the Walmart Visitor Center.

SAM M. WALTON

CHAPTER 3

The Walmart Legend Begins

Walton had to find a new location for his next retail store. He first thought about looking in a big city, but Helen said she wanted to live in another small town like Newport. After some searching, Walton visited the tiny town of Bentonville, Arkansas. There, he found a struggling business called the Harrison Variety Store. Its owners were very happy to sell the store to him.

Walton often located his stores in small towns.

A Place of His Own

Walton fixed up the store to make it more modern. He also bought the barbershop next to it and knocked down the walls in between to make his retail store bigger. He made sure to get a contract so he could stay on the property longer than five years this time. He had learned his lesson from when he got kicked out of Newport! Although the new store was again part of the Ben Franklin chain, Walton decided to call it Walton's Five and Dime.

Walton's Five and Dime was a type of store known as a five-and-ten. They were called this because originally all the items in such stores cost either five or ten cents.

Walmart was one of the first stores of its kind to allow customers to browse and choose products from the shelves.

New Ideas

Walton's store brought many new ideas to the retail business. Almost every other variety store had workers who went around the store picking out items for customers. Customers simply explained what they wanted. Walton felt he could save money by hiring fewer people and allowing customers to walk around the store themselves. Most people were happy with this change. They enjoyed being able to look at other items as they shopped.

Walmart's policy of selling goods at low prices has continued to today.

Walton also believed in selling items at very low prices. If another store sold shoes for five dollars, Walton sold them for four. He didn't make as much money on each pair of shoes, but he sold more of them. Selling more items at a lower cost can often bring in more money than selling expensive items in smaller numbers.

The store soon became a huge success. Walton began buying and opening other stores in the surrounding area. By 1962, he had 16 stores in three states.

The Birth of Walmart

Sam was sure that discounting was the future of retail. He proposed a new line of discount stores to the owners of the Ben Franklin chain, but they weren't interested. Walton decided to join with his brother, Bud, to launch a chain of their own. On July 2, 1962, the brothers opened the very first Walmart in the small town of Rogers, Arkansas. Its name at the time was Walmart Discount City.

The first Walmart, located in Rogers, Arkansas, no longer exists.

Walton stuck to his strategy of low prices. He also advertised sales of everyday items such as soap, shampoo, and toothpaste to bring in customers. The customers would then buy other things, too. The first Walmart was an immediate success. It was soon earning more than $1 million per year. When Sam opened another Walmart in nearby Springdale, it did even better.

Timeline of Sam Walton

1918
Sam Walton is born in Kingfisher, Oklahoma.

1940
Walton starts his first job in retail at J. C. Penney.

1945
Walton purchases a Ben Franklin franchise.

More Stores, Lower Prices

Within five years, Walton had opened 24 Walmarts, and he was buying products from **manufacturers** in huge numbers. This meant he could get the goods at a very low cost and then sell them at prices that were just about impossible to resist. Walton was now a very successful man. He had more than enough money to retire. However, he was only just getting started.

1962
Walton opens the first Walmart in Rogers, Arkansas.

1988
Walton steps down as head of Walmart because of health concerns.

1992
Walton dies of cancer in Little Rock, Arkansas.

Groundbreaking Ideas in Retail

Sam Walton was known for trying new ideas to improve his retail stores. Many of his ideas are now used by other retailers all over the world. Let's take a look at a few of them.

Choosing Your Own Goods

Believe it or not, there was a time when customers didn't really need to shop. They just handed a list to a store clerk, and the clerk collected everything from the shelves. Today, window shopping and browsing through a store are common practices. Sam Walton had a lot to do with that.

Keeping Prices Low

Walton believed that more people would come to his stores if he kept his prices low. He was right! While other retail stores were trying to charge as much as possible, Walton went in the opposite direction. Today, discount chains are located all over the world.

Treating Workers as Business Partners

Walton called his employees "associates" rather than "workers." He wanted them to feel as though his business was also their business. The employees worked hard because they felt a more personal interest in what they were doing.

Making Shopping a Pleasant Experience

Walton made a point of keeping his stores fully stocked and brightly lit. This was a huge difference from many stores that existed when Walmart started. It made the experience of coming into one of Walton's stores much more pleasant.

Big, Bigger, Biggest

Walmart wasn't the only fast-growing discount chain in the United States. The same year that Walton opened his first store, two other chains— Target and Kmart—began doing business. Just as Walton had predicted, discount stores were indeed the wave of the future. By 1967, Kmart was the most successful. Walton had no intention of letting it stay that way.

 The first Kmart discount department store opened in 1962.

During the 1970s, Walton kept traveling around the country looking for new locations. Thanks to his tireless drive to succeed, he opened more than 270 Walmart stores by the end of the decade. Walmart had also begun offering new products, such as auto parts, fine jewelry, and prescription drugs. The company was earning more than $1 billion per year.

Walton visited Walmart stores around the country to make sure they met his standards.

Small business owners sometimes shop at Sam's Club to buy supplies.

Buying Bulk

Sam used his deep-discount approach to open a new chain of stores in the 1980s called Sam's Club. Sam's Club stores offer products in **bulk**. This keeps prices very low. For everyday items such as paper towels or canned goods—things that do not spoil if they sit for a long time—this seems like a good idea to many people. Customers continue to flock to Sam's Club stores by the millions.

The Fall of the Giant

In the early 1980s, Walton began feeling more and more tired every day. He soon went to a doctor and discovered he had a condition called hairy cell leukemia. This is a type of blood cancer that destroys the body's white blood cells. White blood cells help fight off infection and disease. Then Walton's doctor gave him more bad news—most people who have leukemia do not survive for very long.

 Walton continued to work long hours during the early stages of his illness.

Fighting the Good Fight

Walton decided to try a treatment that used a new class of drugs called interferon. He took injections of the drug every day. Within a few months, the leukemia's growth had stopped.

By 1988, Walton was approaching his 70th birthday. Because of his age and his battle against cancer, he didn't have the same energy he'd enjoyed as a young man. He stepped down from the top position of his company and gave control to a team of trusted business executives.

Hairy cell leukemia causes the body to produce abnormal white blood cells.

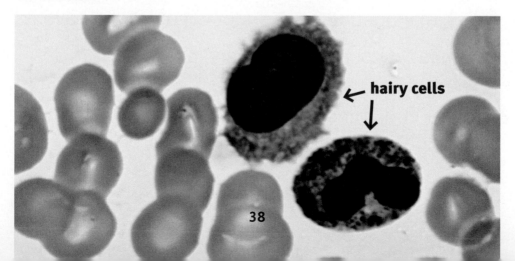

hairy cells

Walton died at the age of 74.

Walton always thought of his employees as partners rather than ordinary workers.

Seven years after Walton's interferon treatment had stopped the growth of his cancer, the disease came back stronger than ever. Walton's doctor told him he had to use more common cancer treatments this time. They slowed the cancer down but could not stop it. On April 5, 1992, Walton died in Little Rock, Arkansas.

Walmart has stores all around the globe, including this one in Hangzhou, China.

Continued Success

Even while Walton knew he was dying, he made plans to ensure that Walmart would continue to grow after he was gone. He handed control of the business over to members of his family and a few business executives. By the end of the 1990s, there were Walmarts in all 50 U.S. states and in several other nations. By the mid-2000s, Walmart had more than 6,000 locations around the world, plus a retail site on the Internet.

Where It All Began

The tiny five-and-dime store that Walton opened in Bentonville, Arkansas, is still there. Today, it serves as the Walmart Visitor Center. It has the original flooring and decorative tin ceiling. The storefront, with its red-and-white-striped awning, hasn't changed either. There is an interactive gallery where the center's 150,000 yearly visitors can follow the Walmart timeline. There is also a café with drinks and snacks—all offered, of course, at discounted prices.

Trouble at the Top

Some people have blamed Walmart for driving smaller mom-and-pop shops out of towns all over the world. Walmart has also been the target of a number of lawsuits, including several accusing the company of unfair business practices and poor treatment of its employees. However, Walmart's new leaders have managed to move the company forward anyway.

Many people have participated in demonstrations against Walmart's practices, arguing that Walmart does not treat its employees fairly.

Sam Walton's influence on retail shopping will likely be felt for many years to come.

Sam Walton was a man of great energy, enthusiasm, and vision. He was never afraid to try new things, and he was never afraid to fail. His attitude was always: "If you try something and it doesn't work, learn from that failure and try something else. But above all else, always try *something*." But perhaps his greatest legacy was that he proved it was possible to start with nothing and make it all the way to the top. ★

True Statistics

Day Sam Walton was born: March 29, 1918

Day Sam Walton died: April 5, 1992

Date the first Walmart opened: July 2, 1962

Number of countries where Walmarts are located today: 27

Annual Walmart sales: About $450 billion

Number of Walmart stores worldwide: More than 10,500

Number of Walmart stores in the United States: Nearly 4,000

Did you find the truth?

(T) Sam Walton once worked for J. C. Penney.

(F) Sam Walton launched the retail chains Walmart, Sam's Club, and Target.

Resources

Books

Dougherty, Terri. *Sam Walton: Department Store Giant*. San Diego: Blackbirch Press, 2004.

Gilbert, Sara. *The Story of Wal-Mart*. Mankato, MN: Creative Paperback, 2012.

Lee, Sally. *Sam Walton: Business Genius of Wal-Mart*. Berkeley Heights, NJ: Enslow Publishers, 2008.

Visit this Scholastic Web site for more information on Sam Walton:
★ www.factsfornow.scholastic.com
Enter the keywords **Sam Walton**

Important Words

bulk (BUHLK) — sold in large quantities, usually for a lower price

chain (CHAYN) — a group of stores that are owned by the same company and sell similar products

economics (ek-uh-NAH-miks) — the study of the way that money, resources, and services are used in a society

expenses (ik-SPEN-siz) — money for a particular job or task, such as paying for a home and food

franchise (FRAN-chize) — a single location of a chain store or restaurant

Great Depression (GRAYT di-PRESH-uhn) — a time when the world economy was shrinking and many people lost their jobs

invest (in-VEST) — to give or lend money to something, such as a company, with the intention of getting more money back later

manufacturers (man-yuh-FAK-chur-urz) — companies that make things

retail (REE-tayl) — having to do with the sale of goods directly to customers

Index

Page numbers in **bold** indicate illustrations

About the Author

Wil Mara is the award-winning author of more than 140 books, many of which are educational titles for young readers.

PHOTOGRAPHS © 2014: Alamy Images: 32 (B. Leighty/Photri Images), cover (Chris Howes/Wild Places Photography), 41 (Dennis MacDonald), 5 top, 24 (Ilene MacDonald), 25 (Jeff Greenberg), 26 (Marjorie Kamys Cotera/Bob Daemmrich Photography), 22, 44 (Terry Smith Images); AP Images: 31 bottom (Andy King), 5 bottom, 34 (Danny Johnston), 31 top (David Zalubowski), 40 (Imaginechina), 42 (J Pat Carter), 30 (John Konstantaras), 4, 35 (Kyle Carter, The Meridian Star), 15 (Peter J. Carroll), 31 center (Ted S. Warren), 36; Bob Italiano: 6; Corbis Images/Bettmann: 8, 20; Flickr/William Warby: cover background; Getty Images: 39 (AFP), back cover (Chris Hondros), 12 (mccannta - Thomas McCann Photography); Library of Congress: 9, 17; Minnesota Historical Society: 14, 18,19; Science Source/Michael Abbey: 38; Seth Poppel Yearbook Library: 10, 11; Shutterstock, Inc./ Kzenon: 30, background, 31 background; Superstock, Inc.: 21 (ClassicStock.com), 16, 28 (Visions of America); Courtesy of Walmart: 27, 29 left; Zuma Press/Robin Nelson: cover inset, 3, 29 right, 43.